RADSPORTS GUIDES

SNOCROSS

TRACY NELSON MAURER

Rourke
Publishing LLC
Vero Beach, Florida 32964

www.rourkepublishing.com

Project Assistance:
Bobby "Rage" LePage, Duluth, MN, signed on with Polaris in 2001 at 16 years of age. A SnoCross champion and FMX/MX rider, he runs anything with a motor—fast. Todd "Starter" LePage and the guys at Duluth Lawn & Sport also contributed their expertise and enthusiasm...again!

Also, the author extends appreciation to the International Snowmobile Manufacturers Association, Blair Morgan Racing Team, Doug Moon, Mike Maurer, and Kendall and Lois M. Nelson.

Photo Credits: Cover: © Allsport; p. 4, 15, 30: © Jamie Squire/Allsport; p. 8, 32, 34: © Al Bello/ Allsport; p.10, 24, 31: © snoxracing.com; p. 11, 27, 38, 41: © Nathan Bilo/Allsport; p. 16, 18, 40: courtesy of Bombardier/Ski-Doo; p. 20: © Corbis; p. 30 © Jamie Squire/Allsport; p. 42: © Bobby LePage

Cover photo: Snocross riders conquer wicked courses with strength, speed, and smart moves.

Editor: Frank Sloan

Cover and page design: Nicola Stratford

Library of Congress Cataloging-in-Publication Data

Maurer, Tracy, 1965-
   Snocross / Tracy Nelson Maurer.
      p. cm. — (Radsports guides)
Summary: Surveys the history, equipment, techniques, and safety factors of snocross.
Includes bibliographical references and index.
   ISBN 1-58952-279-6 (hard)
   1. Snowmobile racing—Juvenile literature. [1. Snowmobile racing.] I.
Title: Sno-cross. II. Title.
   GV856.8 .M39 2002
   796.94—dc21
                                                          2002008227

Printed in the USA

CG/CG

TABLE OF CONTENTS

Racers lean for balance as they fly around the track.

MOTOCROSS, NORTHERN STYLE

You step outside and the bitter cold air freezes your nostrils shut. The wind bites your skin, even under a full-face helmet. The snow is deep enough to bury you alive. Are you having fun yet? For snocross riders and other serious snowmobilers, you're stoked!

chapter
ONE

Snocross, the winter version of motocross, pits snowmobilers and their sleds against nature's wild side. Nasty courses scour solid ice and climb monster hills. **Moguls**, or man-made bumps like motocross whoop-de-doos, become launch pads. Daredevil speed freaks can't resist!

A ROUGH START

In the 1930s, inventors powered sleighs with gear-driven tracks. By the 1950s, the concept of a snow-machine took shape with open, rear-mounted engines. Although the motors often caught fire or blew up, inventors saw promise in the vehicles. In the 1960s, they switched the engine to the front and covered it. The sport took off. Ten years later, the energy crisis stalled it.

By the late 1980s, snowmobiling found new fans. Quieter and more reliable engines, plus cozy options like boot and thumb warmers, attracted family riders. And faster, more powerful machines brought in radical riders looking for big air.

ICE TRACKERS

The sports world didn't pay much attention when the World Championship Snowmobile Derby began back in 1964 in Eagle River, Wisconsin. Now more than 30,000 fans fill the grandstands every year for the biggest event in ice-oval track snowmobile racing.

In ice-ovals, up to eight sleds usually run 40 laps for a race. They gun their throttles at the green flag. Ice chips hurl from the sled tracks digging for **traction**.

Ripping into the turns, skilled drivers brake carefully at just the right time. Too much speed or an inch too far up or down on the sloped corners can mean sliding off the course. Nailing it can mean victory.

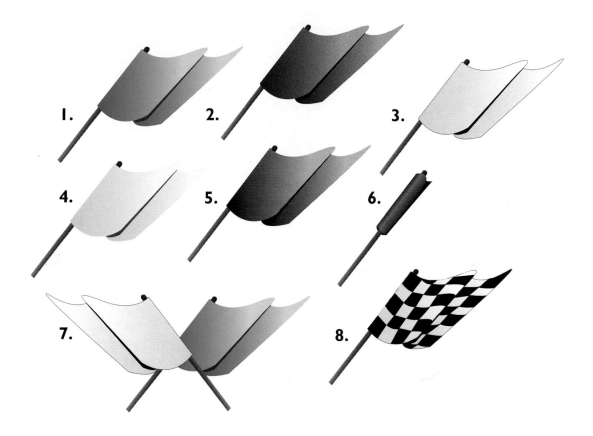

FLAG CODES

Every racetrack uses colored flags to signal drivers. If you want to race, know the code.

1. Green = Go
2. Red = Stop racing or restart
3. White = One lap left
4. Yellow = Caution; do not pass in the accident area
5. Open Black = Disqualified driver
6. Rolled-up Black = Violation warning; stop and wait for green flag
7. Crossed White and Green = Half way
8. Checkered = End of race

Racers hammer their throttles at the starting line to catch an early lead.

SLED-HEADS

Thanks to the Winter X Games, snocross now dominates the snowmobiling race scene. Winning sled-heads gain fame and even a bit of fortune at Winter X. Some sponsors, mostly the machine manufacturers, offer big bonus bucks to their Winter X champs.

Snocross delivers non-stop action. Unlike ice-ovals, this snow-covered course makes a large loop that rumbles over moguls, pitched banks, tabletop jumps, and other insane terrain.

HAMMER DOWN FOR THE HOLESHOT

Up to 14 drivers hammer their throttles at the snocross starting line. The **holeshot**, or the lead position at the start, keeps that racer ahead of sled traffic.

As the racers rocket through the 8- to 12-lap course, they grind against each other. They lock skis. They fight to keep their line, or route, over the course.

Fans love to watch the machines fly off bumps. But big air can slow a machine down. Most riders try to stay low unless they can gain distance off a jump or pass another racer.

RAD TRIVIA

No Show Snow
The show goes on, even without snow. Race organizers may spend tens of thousands of dollars to make or haul in snow.

REVVED UP, UP, UP

Hillcross works like snocross except a herd of ten machines charge straight up a steep course. Riders bounce off moguls as they climb. Some bounce backward. They land in a heap at the bottom. The fastest racer to reach the top wins.

A hillclimb race puts just one machine at a time on the course. The rider to the peak with the fastest time wins. Speed matters, but most riders simply try to finish. Most don't. You can find the loser machines by following their trails of broken windshields, cowls, handlebars, and other parts and pieces.

MORE EXTREMELY EXTREME RIDING

Hillclimbers aren't alone in the extremely extreme class. In water-cross, racers run their sleds over open rivers and lakes. Losers sink.

Hillclimbers race to the peak, fighting gravity all the way.

Cross-country races can last for days and travel over fields, ice, woodlands, mountains, and other terrain.

Drag races on ice, snow, asphalt, and even grass cover a straight course that's just 600 feet (183 m) to one-quarter mile (402 m) long. The machines roar in a sprint that determines the winner by fractions of a second.

Opposite of drags, cross-country races run for days, sometimes covering more than 1,000 miles (1,609 km). About 100 riders in each race test their strength and endurance over all kinds of terrain.

Nearly all snowmobiling events today feature freestyle big air and jumping contests, too. Even the 2002 Winter Olympics in Salt Lake City stepped up with an exhibition. You'll see the same sick tricks that motocross riders throw, like heel-clickers and supermans, plus some new moves just for snowmobiles.

SKILLS BEFORE THRILLS

Riding snowmobiles, like driving cars, takes some skill. You need to know your state's laws, too. Most require drivers to take approved classes even if you only joy-ride and never race. Ask your snowmobile dealer for information about safety classes. The dealer can also tell you how to register or license your machine.

If you're between ages 5 and 9, you might start racing on Arctic Cat Kitty Cats. These real machines look like big sleds in mini size. Ages 10 to 13 move up to the Junior Novice division, but they can ride only certain models that top out at 40 miles (64.4 km) per hour. From ages 14 to 16, racers ride stock machines in the Junior or Sport Class. These classes fill up the fastest.

RAD TRIVIA

OEM Sleds
Many races for kids require Original Equipment Manufacturer (OEM) sleds, or stock snowmobiles. You can't install operating parts made by a different factory on an OEM sled. Read your race rules carefully!

RACING SLEDS

Sleds don't come cheap. A Pro Open machine, built with non-stock parts for speed, can easily cost $35,000. You should start with a stock machine. Fortunately, they cost a lot less—about $5,800 new.

Only four manufacturers rule the industry: Arctic Cat and Polaris Industries, both in Minnesota, Yamaha Motor Corporation USA in California, and Bombardier (Ski-Doo) in Canada. These four factories also sponsor snowmobile race teams.

chapter

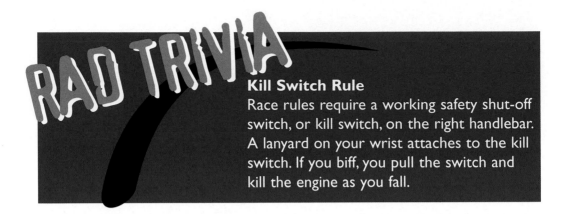

Kill Switch Rule
Race rules require a working safety shut-off switch, or kill switch, on the right handlebar. A lanyard on your wrist attaches to the kill switch. If you biff, you pull the switch and kill the engine as you fall.

A SLED OF YOUR OWN

Every year, U.S. snowmobile dealers sell more than 100,000 new sleds. About 1.6 million sleds are registered in this country, improving your odds of finding a used one for sale in the newspaper and sports shops. Check carefully for engine and track wear. Bring in a mechanic if you're not sure.

Like motorcycles, snowmobiles come with different size engines measured in cubic centimeters (cc). Today, most riders buy sleds in the 500-cc class. Every motor uses either liquid or air for cooling. Air-cooled engines cost less. They work fine until the weather warms up to 30° F (minus 1° C).

RACING ENGINES

Engine size sets the race classes. The 440 fan-cooled engine, usually the smallest racing choice, reaches up to 80 miles (129 km) per hour. Open-mod 1000s are the most powerful engines. They clock at over 150 miles (245 km) per hour.

Starting with Sport class, racing classes divide by engine type. "Sport 600 Stock" means a race with OEM engines no larger than 600cc. Formula I sleds race against Formula I; Formula III machines race against Formula III.

The sled you buy depends on how and where you ride. Lightweight machines easily handle throttle changes on twisty wooded trails. Heavier, more powerful sleds do better running wide open in events like drags or oval races with few speed changes.

Racing classes divide by the size and type of engine and also by the age of the rider.

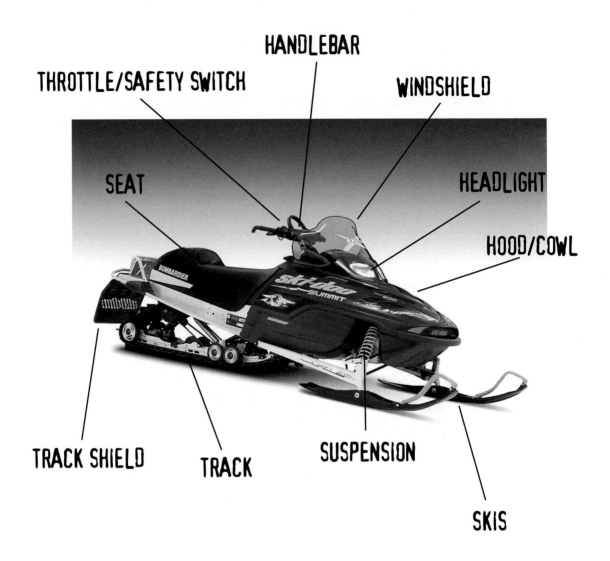

HANDLEBAR

THROTTLE/SAFETY SWITCH

WINDSHIELD

SEAT

HEADLIGHT

HOOD/COWL

TRACK SHIELD

TRACK

SUSPENSION

SKIS

Some parts every rider should know.

TOOL TIME

Remember the owner's manual that came with your machine? Read it. Then read it again. Some machines use a special mix of oil and gasoline. Mess up there, and you fry the engine.

Tape the "pre-op" check list to your garage wall. Before each session, or ride, make sure you and your machine are ready. Regular maintenance between sessions also avoids hauling your dead sled out of the woods.

PART BY PART

If you plan to race, know your machine part by part. Memorize the rules for your racing class before you turn a wrench. What if you sharpened the carbide strip on your skis and didn't read the rules? Most races would toss you out.

Learn how to trouble-shoot so you can fix problems when you're riding. Hang out with the mechanics at the dealership. Ask them questions.

Check what's legal for trail riding in your state, too. Some states ban metal studs on your track. Some have age limits. Even if you race, you'll still ride with buddies. Ride legal.

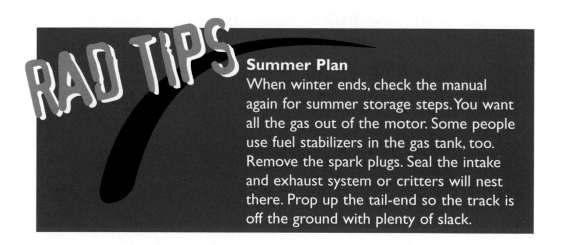

RAD TIPS

Summer Plan
When winter ends, check the manual again for summer storage steps. You want all the gas out of the motor. Some people use fuel stabilizers in the gas tank, too. Remove the spark plugs. Seal the intake and exhaust system or critters will nest there. Prop up the tail-end so the track is off the ground with plenty of slack.

BATTLE ARMOR

Snocross riders battle for position on open sleds. Most races require a closed-face helmet, a safety jacket, shin pads, goggles, over-the-ankle boots, and **reinforced** pants. Racers also use elbow and knee pads. They wear thick, snowboard-style gloves, too. Many racers stick wide strips of tape on their noses and chins to stop the wind from ripping the skin open.

Not racing? ALWAYS wear your helmet anyway.

Underneath the racing gear, layer your clothes. Start with clothing that wicks sweat away from your body. If you're doing tricks, especially tricks with the handlebars, don't forget some extra protection for your privates. Next, wear fleece and not cotton. Cotton can trap sweat, which freezes into an icy glaze over your skin. Choose a wind-proof outer layer.

REINFORCED PANTS AND JACKET

HELMET

EYE PROTECTION

FACE GUARD

PADDED GLOVES

HIGH-TOP BOOTS

WHAT MORE DO YOU NEED?

Sleds are heavy beasts. Racing machines weigh a minimum of 350 pounds (159 kg) dry. Instead of lugging them around the garage or onto the trailer, try one of the special wheeled dollies for sale in the after-market catalogs or on the Web. Save your strength for sessions!

If you live in the city or far from a trail, you'll also need a pick-up truck with a ramp or a trailer.

Check with a local dealer, police, or the Department of Natural Resources for your state about registering the sled. The American Council of Snowmobile Associations (ACSA) also keeps tabs on state laws. You probably need registration decals, or stickers, on each side of the cowl. You might also have to carry proof that you completed a safety course. Fines and jail-time stink.

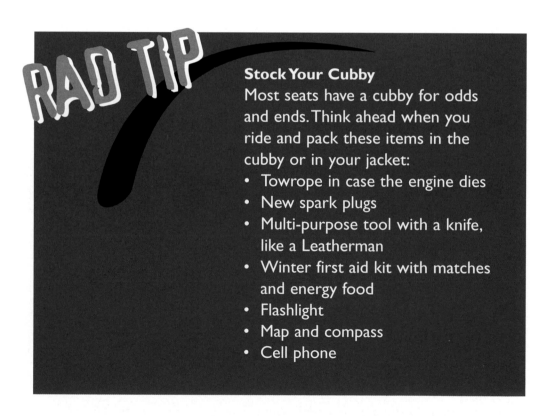

RAD TIP

Stock Your Cubby
Most seats have a cubby for odds and ends. Think ahead when you ride and pack these items in the cubby or in your jacket:
- Towrope in case the engine dies
- New spark plugs
- Multi-purpose tool with a knife, like a Leatherman
- Winter first aid kit with matches and energy food
- Flashlight
- Map and compass
- Cell phone

SHAPE UP

Snocross drivers use their weight to lean into curves. Some drivers stand, lap after lap. Others stand and sit, stand and sit. Some kneel and others sit with their feet locked into the **footwells**.

Whatever your style, your body takes a pounding. Develop strength, balance, and **endurance** to stay in the game.

Follow a training routine and eat healthy food all year. Build your upper-body strength so you can wrestle the sled where you want it. Lift weights and do push-ups (they say you can never do too many push-ups). Prime your **quadriceps**, or thighs, too. Lunges and squats build power and endurance in your legs.

Before a race, warm up for ten minutes with an easy jog. Then stretch slowly.

Cross-train in the summer with motocross, personal watercraft riding, mountain biking, or in-line skating.

THROTTLE THINKING

Before your thumb jabs down on the throttle, rev up your brain. The world has enough stupid drivers already. Know the risks.

Every session brings different **hazards**. During the day, glare off the snow can blind you. At night, tail-lights ahead can **disorient** you. Weather conditions and trail or race course conditions can change quickly. Think ahead. And think it through.

chapter

THREE

HANDLEBAR HANDLING

Before you hop on your sled, let somebody know where you're going and when you'll be back. Search-teams hate false alarms. Ride with a buddy. If you biff, you have someone to drive you to the hospital.

THE SLEDDER'S PLEDGE

- I will drive within the limits of my machine and my own abilities.
- I will obey the rules and laws of the state or province I am visiting.
- I will be careful when crossing roads, and always cross at a right angle to traffic.
- I will keep my machine in top shape and follow a pre-op check before each ride.
- I will wear appropriate clothing, including gloves, boots, and a helmet with a visor.
- I will let family or friends know my planned route, my destination, and my expected arrival time.
- I will treat the outdoors with respect. I will not litter or damage trees or other vegetation.
- I will respect other peoples' property and rights, and lend a hand when I see someone in need.
- I will not snowmobile where prohibited.

Courtesy of the International Snowmobile Manufacturers Association

Snow can make your visibility very poor so always ride with a safe stopping distance between your machines.

How you handle your sled impacts your arrival condition. Watch your speed. Some states have trail speed limits (and cops on snowmobiles to issue tickets). Keep some space between you and the rider ahead of you, too. You need about 300 feet (91.4 m), almost the length of a football field, to stop a sled traveling 50 miles (80.5 km) per hour.

Since the sled-head behind you can't stop on a dime, use hand signals when you turn.
- Left turn: left arm extended straight out
- Right turn: left arm out, forearm raised, with elbow at 90-degree angle
- Stop: left arm raised straight up
- Slow: left arm out and angled toward ground

Inside your helmet, roaring sounds from the engine and wind drown out the sound of train whistles and honking horns. Cross railroad tracks, paved roads, and **recreation** trails only after you stop and check both ways.

Wearing the right safety gear protects racers when they crash on the track. Trail riders must always wear a helmet for safety, too.

DON'T TAKE THE PLUNGE

Avoid crossing frozen lakes and rivers. If that's not **realistic** where you live, then learn to call the DNR or police for the ice conditions and thickness reports. Sound dweeby? Drowning causes most snowmobile deaths.

Remember that currents in rivers create soft spots. Lakes are not wide-open runways. Branches, docks, and other surprises freeze into ice. Crashes with other sleds happen too often out there.

If you plunge under the ice, stay focused. Kick for the surface. Keep your gloves on to help you grab the ice. If the ice breaks when you pull up, move toward shallow water. Once you're up, roll far away from the hole.

RAD FACT

Hypothermia Isn't Hype
Hypothermia starts with shivering. Don't wait! Warm up indoors and sip warm water or tea. You might feel cranky, sleepy, or dazed. Some victims pass out. Hypothermia can even kill.

ALTITUDE ATTITUDE

Riding in mountain snow country cranks up the fun. It's also more dangerous. Give yourself at least a day to adjust to the **altitude**. Altitude sickness can make you woozy and ready to hurl your lunch. It can do worse, too.

Ride alert everywhere you go, but especially in the mountains. Cliffs, fences, trees, rocks, farm animals, and deer make painful targets. Avoid them. Stay out of **avalanche** zones, too. Those powdery waterfalls look awesome on TV, but they're deadly. Carry a **transceiver**, or beep, shovel and probe pole with your regular safety gear.

GREAT WHITE FREEWAYS

More than 225,000 miles (362,093 km) of groomed and marked snowmobile trails become the great white freeways of North America during the winter. About 40,000 miles (63,472 km) of them are managed under the U.S. Department of Agriculture on National Forest land, often groomed and marked by volunteers.

Stay on the marked trails. Private landowners pitch a fit when snowmobilers stray into their pastures, gardens, and lawns. Many angry landowners take back **access rights** then. Respect private property and all of the outdoors. Thrashing the trails ruins the sport for everyone.

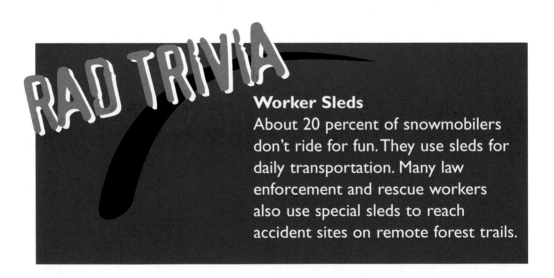

RAD TRIVIA

Worker Sleds
About 20 percent of snowmobilers don't ride for fun. They use sleds for daily transportation. Many law enforcement and rescue workers also use special sleds to reach accident sites on remote forest trails.

Mountain riding amps up the excitement. Always check the avalanche and weather forecasts before you go.

THE GROOMSMEN

After most snowmobilers are tucked in bed for the night, grooming machines begin to slowly crawl along the dark trails. These huge, lumbering machines tow special metal **drags** behind them to smooth the bumps and ridges churned up by packs of snowmobilers.

Most groomers are volunteers from local snowmobile clubs. The clubs work with their area's government agencies to mark and maintain the trails. Some clubs receive money for their work, but it's never enough to cover the full cost of keeping the trails open, safe, and smooth.

Always thank those busy volunteers and stay out of their way.

RAD TRIVIA

Drags
Snowmobile clubs buy their bulky grooming machines new and used from ski hills. They also buy different drags to smooth the trails in various snow and weather conditions.

WE HAVE LIFT-OFF

Changes in sled design helped the sport reach new heights—and big air. Better speed, power, and handling by the 1990s gave freestyle pilots more control over the machines.

Your owner's manual probably explains that YOUR SLED WAS NOT BUILT FOR JUMPING. It's true. Freestyle riding pushes the machine beyond its purpose. Only the most advanced riders should try for the sky.

chapter

FOUR

If you wipe out on your machine, try and push away from it.

OVER THE EDGE

Freestyle snowmobiling borrows a lot of tricks from freestyle motocross. The whip you see in motocross works about the same way on a snowmobile. Sno-pilots push their sleds sideways to the landing, like a "T," in the air. Then they straighten in time for the landing.

Riding on your sled's tail with the skis in the air looks like an easy wheelie. It's not. Like all tricks, it takes practice. And practice. And practice. It also takes huge guts and an attitude that's over the edge.

BIFF AND BAIL

Serious riders biff. A lot. The goal is to climb back up again and ride better next time. Try to bail safely. When you fall off your sled, push your body away. Keep rolling away from the machine with your arms guarding your head. Even with a kill switch, the spinning track may whip parts and pieces at you.

Remember this ditty: Land flat, break your back. Most landings come in tail first, then down on the nose. That works best. Nose-first landings often fling you over the handlebars.

Ride Loose
Keep your knees loose when you jump to absorb the landing impact. Think of wet, cooked spaghetti noodles. Throw them at the wall and they handle the impact. Dry, stiff noodles break.

Never go down with your machine. It outweighs you by a couple hundred pounds and can do serious damage if it lands on you.

"Go big!" say the freestyle riders. And they do—launching for major air. Freestyle snowmobiling borrows a lot of tricks from freestyle motocross.

AIR SHOWS

The freestyle side of snowmobiling rips with full-throttle attitude. Sno-pilots ride for maximum **adrenaline** rush, but not for too many big-buck prizes. Organized competitions with judges, **podiums**, and rules are rare—so far. Invitational snowmobile freestyle contests usually piggyback with other events, like the World Championship Hillclimbs.

Riders like Ryan Britt, Chris Burandt, and Andy Lindbeck live to grab big air wherever they can. Mostly, you see them slashing the slopes in jaw-dropping freestyle videos.

When you see them ride, remember that they don't drive beater sleds. They **modify** their rides with higher handlebars, wider running boards, and engine upgrades.

HIGH FLIERS

Before you try airborne moves, dial in your jumps. You should feel comfortable with catching air and landing. Scope out your landing zone before you fly, too.

Freestyle is all about style: slow, smooth, even control in the air and lots of flair. Hold tricks as long as you can to really show your style.

Every trick described here is dangerous and difficult. Only advanced riders should try to fly.

Again, ALWAYS wear a helmet.

Heel clickers look easy, but they take practice.

THE HEEL CLICKER

You probably see more heel clickers than any other move. Even the snocross racers will throw a happy heel clicker at the finish line.

To do a heel clicker, look for a good-sized jump with decent air-time potential. You need time to haul your legs over the handlebars and pull them back before you land.

Hit the jump base with hot speed. As you leave the lip, hold on tightly to the handlebars. Kick your feet up and out from the running boards.

Tap your brakes very lightly to level the sled if you need to.

With your arms straight, push your hind-end back and open your legs wide. Catching the windshield or bars ruins the trick and hurts, too. Try to click your heels together in the air. Then quickly kick your feet back out and down to the running boards.

Stay standing for the landing. Keep your knees loose when you stick it.

THE CANDY BAR AND THE SARAN WRAP

Look for a medium-size jump. You want a smooth take-off and a downhill landing.

Some sno-pilots work up to the Saran wrap from the candy bar. With a candy bar, one foot stretches out through your arms and over the handlebars. Pull your leg back through and kick it down.

The Saran wrap takes the same idea and adds style. Instead of just pulling your foot back through, sweep your leg over the handlebar as you lift your hand off that side. Wrap your leg back down and put both hands on the bars for the landing.

Keep the move smooth for maximum style.

THE SUPERMAN SEAT GRAB

Before you try this seat grab, build a strap onto your frame or in the seat. A loop of sturdy hose bolted on the side of your tunnel works well. Test it on solid ground first. Really crank on the hose to make sure it holds you.

Find a smooth jump that delivers decent air-time. Practice in stages. First, just slide back and grab the strap with both hands while you're in the air. When you dial that move in, add a no-footer so that you kick both feet out to the sides. Practice until you feel smooth. Then move to a full-body stretch. Try to keep your body level so your sled stays level, too.

Use the strap to pull yourself up and onto the sled. Spot the landing and stick it like a hero.

Large crowds now turn out to see the pros.

EXTREME SCENE

In the late 1990s and early 2000s, Old Man Winter hit a dry spell across some of the major snowmobile areas. Casual cruisers and Sunday snowmobile drivers couldn't ride, so they watched instead.

Snocross crowds grew by the thousands, bringing ESPN with them. Televised events still draw solid ratings, especially when they feature freestyle air shows. Now events like the Super Snowcross Stadium Tour pamper the dedicated snowmobiling race fans. Men and women alike cheer for their favorite riders in warm, indoor comfort. Wimps.

chapter

FIVE

JOIN THE CREW

Sanctioned by International Snowmobile Racing (ISR), the World Snowmobiling Association (WSA) organizes ten regional races with snocross events that lead to Winter X Game qualification. Only WSA members can race the group's **circuit**.

The Canadian Snocross Racing Association (CSRA) also sanctions snocross events, including those held at Eagle River. Again, to race with CSRA, you must join the organization.

Usually any snocross event asks potential racers to complete an application form, sign an injury waiver, and pay an entrance fee. If you're under 18, your parents have to sign, too. The bigger events may also ask you for your race history, including the classes you raced in and what places you won. Prize-money races or freestyle contests may invite certain big-name riders to help attract crowds.

A PRO JOB

Look at a snocross crowd and the factory colors pop out. Arctic Cat fans wear purple and green. Ski-Doo loyalists dress in yellow. Polaris people put on red. Yamaha fans wear blue.

When you sign with a factory team, you show your colors best by clinching the black-and-white flag. You might not sign with a factory team. Some teams are sponsored by non-factory companies, such as Amsoil. Racers can change teams and sleds, and many of them do. They have agents who help them make deals.

A Ski-Doo rider

Along the way, riders sign with other product sponsors. They slap product graphics all over their machines. It's part of the job. Going pro means you work for your sponsors by advertising for them.

Many racers dream of riding for a factory team.

NAMES TO KNOW

You probably don't know Bobby "The Rage" LePage. Not yet, anyway.

Like many teen-age racers, LePage lives to ride. He practices every day after school, studies other racers, and works on his machines. The hard work is already paying off. He signed with Polaris in 2001 and earned the WSA Overall Point Champion title in his class that year.

Young racers practice many long hours to move up to the big competitions.

Now, you may have heard of Blair "Superman" Morgan. But nobody knew his name when he started out. Today, Morgan ranks among the sport's best with more than 50 outdoor national titles, two indoor snocross point championships, and gold medals at Winter X. His main rival? Chris "Air" Vincent. These two riders carve the fastest lines on the track and nail the sickest tricks.

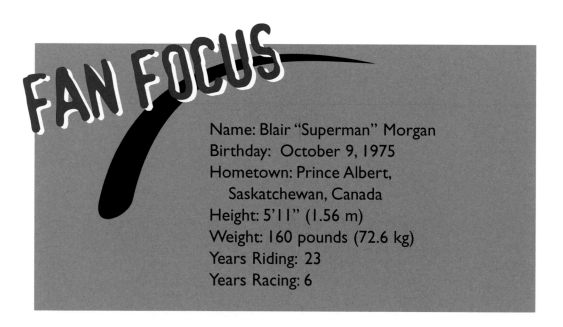

FAN FOCUS

Name: Blair "Superman" Morgan
Birthday: October 9, 1975
Hometown: Prince Albert,
    Saskatchewan, Canada
Height: 5'11" (1.56 m)
Weight: 160 pounds (72.6 kg)
Years Riding: 23
Years Racing: 6

RIDE, RIDE, RIDE

Sled-heads think snowmobiles make winter worthwhile. You don't have to race or ride freestyle to jam on a sled!

Take your time and enjoy the sport. It's good exercise and an excellent excuse for cruising through the woods.

If you want to learn more about snocross or freestyle snowmobiling, visit your library or the Web. Try to catch a live event. Otherwise, ask at the video store to see some of the most extreme snowmobiling ever.

Most importantly, ride safely, ride often, and have fun!

FURTHER READING

SnowWeek Magazine

Snowmobile Magazine

SnowGoer Magazine

William P. Mara. *Snowmobile Racing,* Capstone Press,
    Mankato, MN, 1999.

VIDEOS

Slednecks Y2K, produced by Peak Productions, 2000.

Snow Motion II, produced by Petersen/Riverbend Films, 1999.

WEBSITES TO VISIT

www.expn.com

www.ExtremeSports.com

www.driftjumper.com

www.slednecks.com

www.snowmobile.org

www.snowmobileacsa.org

snowmobilenews.com

www.wsaracing.com

GLOSSARY

access rights (AK ses RIHTS) — the privilege to use someone's
    land or property

adrenaline (ah DREN ul in) — a body chemical released when the
    person is startled, afraid, or excited

altitude (AL tih tood) — height, especially the distance from sea
    level on earth

avalanche (AV uh lanch) — a large area of snow that breaks free and
    plows down the mountain like a mud slide

circuit (SUR kit) — in racing, the schedule or tour of races for
    the season

disorient (dis OR ee ent) — to confuse, or to cause a person to
    become lost

drags (DRAGZ) — in snowmobile grooming, grooming machines tow
    this metal equipment to smooth and shape the trail

endurance (en DOOR ans) — ability to keep going

footwells (FOOT welz) — on a snowmobile, the forward positions
    on the machine's running boards for the driver's feet

hazards (HAZ ardz) — risks or dangers
holeshot (HOHL shot) — the lead position at the start of a race

modify (MOD uh fih) — to change or upgrade

moguls (MOH gulz) — bumps carved in the snow

podiums (POH dee umz) — small platforms where winners
are recognized

quadriceps (KWAD reh seps) — muscles on the top side of
the thighs

realistic (REE uh LIS tik) — practical, sensible

recreation (rek ree AY shun) — fun, not work

reinforced (ree in FORSD) — made stronger

traction (TRAK shun) — the ability of a foot or wheel to grip the
terrain or surface

transceiver (tran SEE vur) — a small safety radio that sends out
beeps to rescue workers

INDEX

ABOUT THE AUTHOR

Tracy Nelson Maurer specializes in nonfiction and business writing. Her most recently published children's books include the *Radsports I* series, also from Rourke Publishing LLC. She lives with her husband Mike and two children in Superior, Wisconsin.